THAT'S STRANGE!

THE HAUNTED STANLEY HOTEL

Tim Cooke

Lerner Publications ◆ Minneapolis

Copyright © 2025 by Lerner Publishing Group, Inc.

All rights reserved. International copyright secured. No part of this book may be reproduced, stored in a retrieval system, or transmitted in any form or by any means—electronic, mechanical, photocopying, recording, or otherwise—without the prior written permission of Lerner Publishing Group, Inc., except for the inclusion of brief quotations in an acknowledged review.

Lerner Publications Company
An imprint of Lerner Publishing Group, Inc.
241 First Avenue North
Minneapolis, MN 55401 USA

For reading levels and more information, look up this title at www.lernerbooks.com.

Main body text set in ITC Franklin Gothic.
Typeface provided by International Typeface Corporation.

Library of Congress Cataloging-in-Publication Data

Names: Cooke, Tim, 1961–author.
Title: The haunted Stanley Hotel / Tim Cooke.
Description: Minneapolis : Lerner Publications, [2025] | Series: That's strange! Updog Books | Includes bibliographical references and index. | Audience: Ages 8–11 | Audience: Grades 4–6 |
Summary: "Guests at the Stanley Hotel in Colorado claim the building is haunted. It even inspired a famous book! Readers will learn more about the strange occurrences, and whether they are true"—Provided by publisher.
Identifiers: LCCN 2024015119 (print) | LCCN 2024015120 (ebook) | ISBN 9798765648216 (lib. bdg.) | ISBN 9798765662557 (pbk.) | ISBN 9798765658994 (epub)
Subjects: LCSH: Stanley Hotel (Estes Park, Colo.)—Juvenile literature. | Haunted hotels—Colorado—Estes Park—Juvenile literature. | CYAC: Haunted places—Colorado—Estes Park—Juvenile literature.
Classification: LCC BF1474.5 .C66 2025 (print) | LCC BF1474.5 (ebook) | DDC 133.1/29097881—dc23/eng/20240508

LC record available at https://lccn.loc.gov/2024015119
LC ebook record available at https://lccn.loc.gov/2024015120

Manufactured in the United States of America

1 – CG – 12/15/24

Table of Contents

Haunted! 4

Unusual Events 10

Scary Fourth Floor 18

What's Going On? 24

Glossary 30

Check It Out! 31

Index 32

Haunted!

4

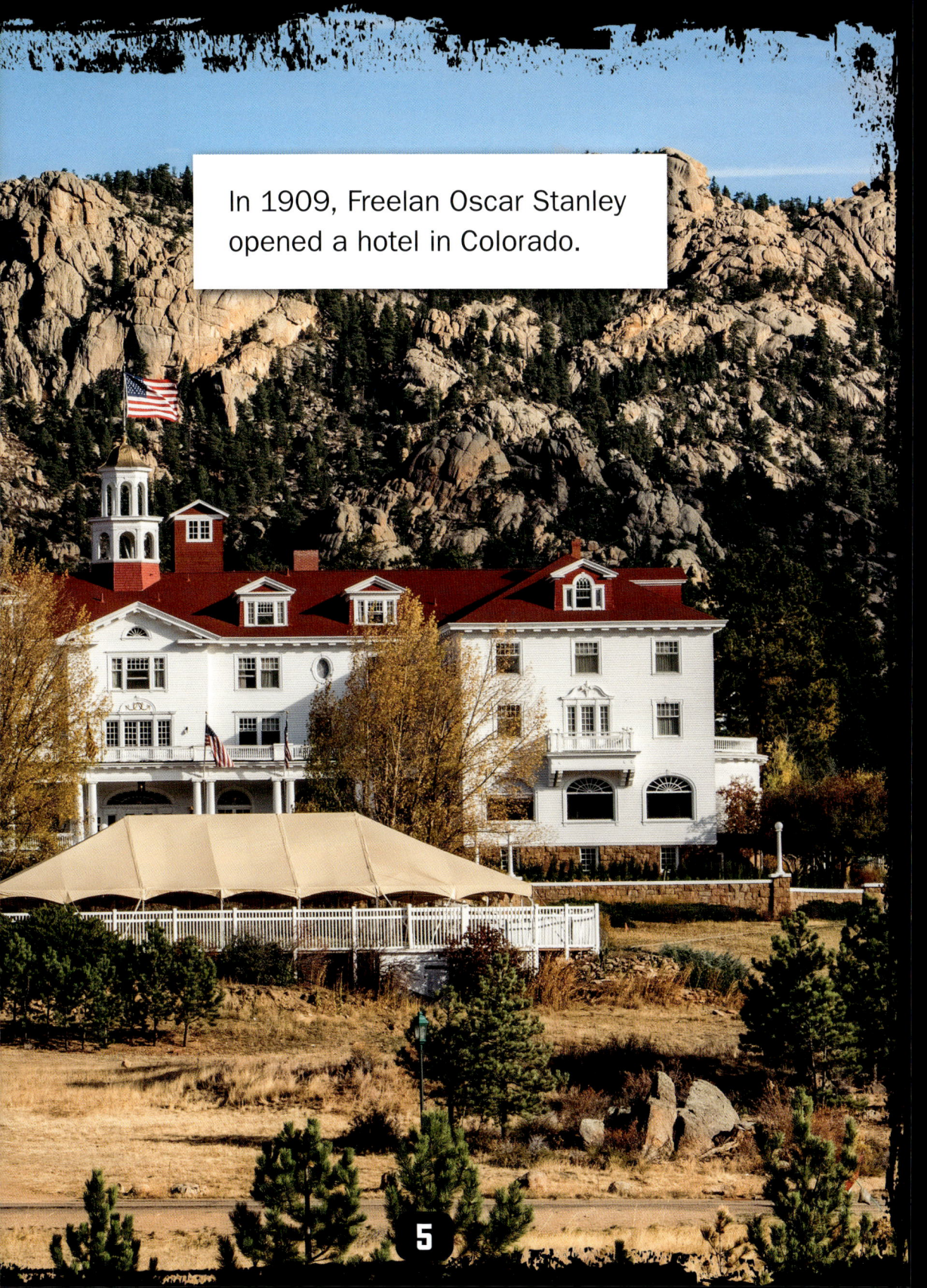

In 1909, Freelan Oscar Stanley opened a hotel in Colorado.

Staircase

People came from all over to stay in the hotel.

It was only open in the summer. In the winter, there was too much snow.

Strange things started to happen. An explosion blew out the floor in a bedroom.

A maid had been lighting a lantern.

UP NEXT!

SCARY STORIES.

Unusual Events

Strange things happened in the hotel. Guests heard the hotel's piano playing at night when no one was near it.

Bedrooms felt cold when the heat was on.

In 1974 a writer stayed at the hotel with his family.

They were the only guests.

The writer wrote about the hotel in a famous horror book.

People believed the Stanley Hotel was haunted.

List Break!

Other famous haunted places include:

St. Augustine Lighthouse in Florida

San Fernando Cathedral in San Antonio, Texas

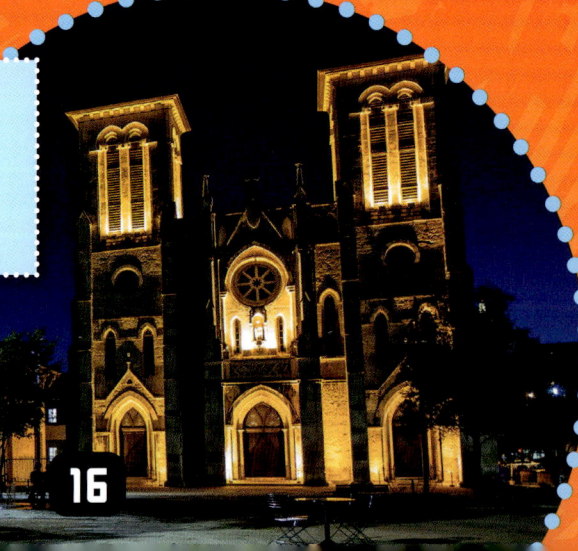

Lincoln Park Zoo in Chicago, Illinois

UP NEXT!

HAUNTED ROOMS.

Scary Fourth Floor

People think the fourth floor is haunted.

Guests say they hear furniture moving.

Some people hear children laughing. Others feel that a small boy plays with their hair.

In one room, guests are tucked into bed against their will.

Some people going to sleep say a friendly cowboy watches them.

Hotel armchair

Others report chairs and windows moving on their own.

UP NEXT!

A MYSTERY.

What's Going On?

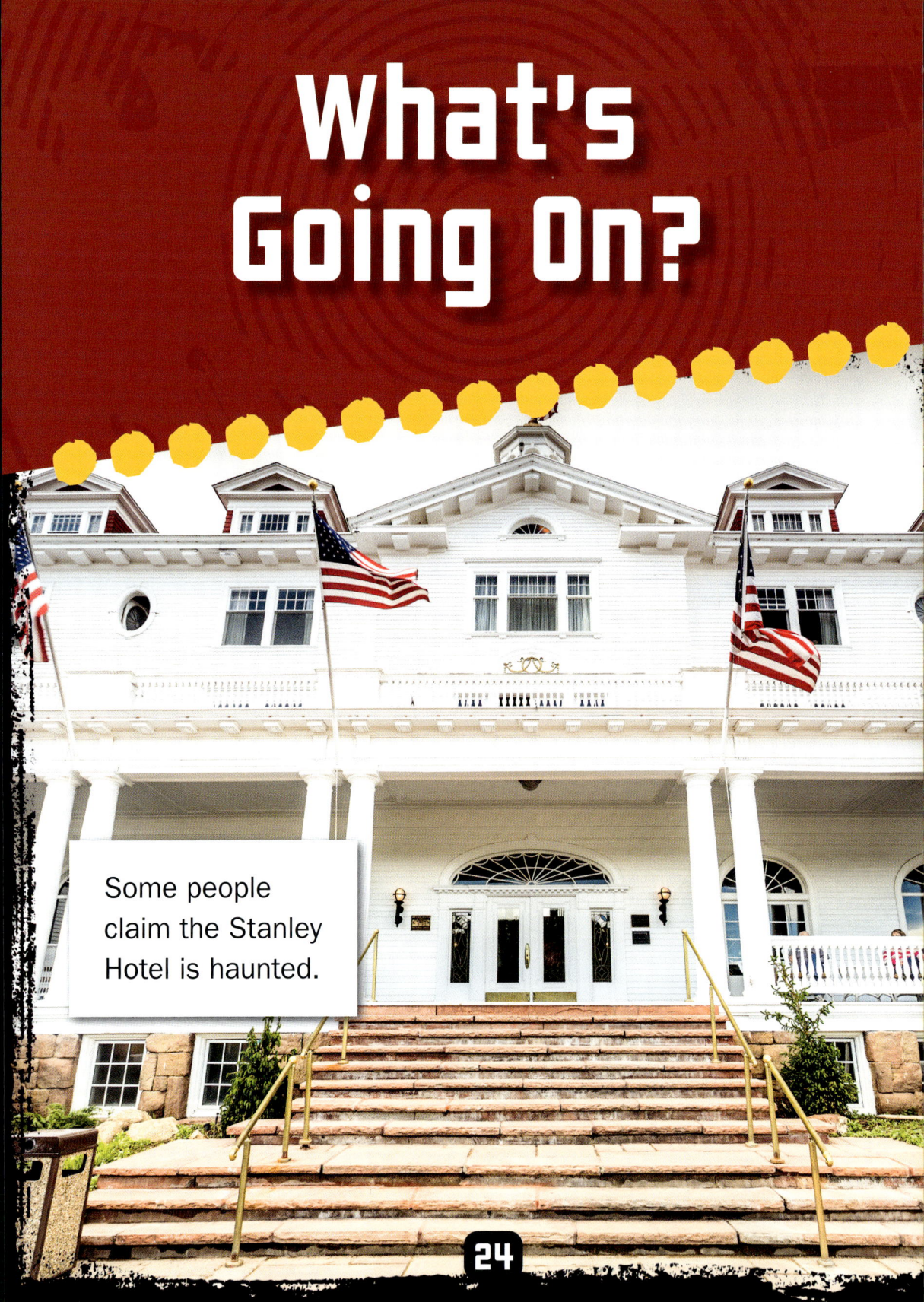

Some people claim the Stanley Hotel is haunted.

They say the strange events are caused by the ghosts of dead people.

Ghost hunters have studied the hotel.

No one can explain the strange activity.

What is behind the creepy hotel?

Do animals move around the rooms at night? Or could it be the people who work there?

Glossary

creepy: frightening and unpleasant

explosion: a sudden loud burst of energy

ghost: the spirit of a dead person

haunted: being home to ghosts

horror: meant to shock and scare people

Check It Out!

Academic Kids: Ghosts
https://academickids.com/encyclopedia/index.php/Ghosts

Carlson-Berne, Emma. *Ghost Hunters*. Minneapolis: Lerner Books, 2024.

Kiddle: Haunted Houses
https://kids.kiddle.co/Haunted_house

Kiddle: The Stanley Hotel
https://kids.kiddle.co/The_Stanley_Hotel

Lassieur, Allison. *Stanley Hotel: A Chilling Interactive Adventure*. North Mankato, MN: Capstone Press, 2017.

Lukidis, Lydia. *Haunted Hotels*. Mankato, MN: Black Rabbit Books, 2021

Index

Colorado, 5

ghost hunters, 26
ghosts, 25

haunted, 15–16, 18, 24

writer, 12, 14

Photo Acknowledgments

Image credits: Kit Leong/Shutterstock, pp. 3, 6, 15; Phillip Rubino/Shutterstock, pp. 4–5; Peter Bowman/Shutterstock, p. 7; Frame Stock Footage/Shutterstock, p. 8; Olivier Le Queinec/Shutterstock, p. 9; Flickr.com/Wikimedia Commons, p. 10; Bianco Blue/Dreamstime.com, p. 11; Different Seasons (1982) back cover, first edition/Wikimedia Commons, p. 12; Kaul Photo and Cinema/Shutterstock, p. 13; Michele Brusini/ Shutterstock, p. 14; Mary Terriberry/Shutterstock, p. 16 (top); CrackerClips Stock Media/Shutterstock, p. 16 (bottom); Jim Roberts/Dreamstime.com, p. 17; Alain P/Shutterstock, p. 18; Alexandre Zveiger /Dreamstime.com, p. 19; Vika200581/Dreamstime.com, p. 20; Darryl Brooks/Dreamstime.com, p. 21; Bob Pool/Shutterstock, p. 22; Tohid Hashemkhani/Shutterstock, p. 23 (top); hupeng/Dreamstime.com, p. 23 (bottom); Sopotnicki/Shutterstock, p. 24; zef art/Shutterstock, p. 25; kinomaster/Dreamstime.com, p. 26; Paul Brady/Dreamstime.com, p. 27; Darla Hallmark/Dreamstime.com, p. 28; Stacy Jenkins/Dreamstime.com. Design elements: sokolovski/Shutterstock, pp. 1–32.

Cover: sokolovski/Shutterstock; Peter Bowman/Shutterstock; I B Photography/Shutterstock.